The Wonderful World of Colour

COLOUR IN ANIMALS

SALLY AND ADRIAN MORGAN

Evans Brothers Limited

Published by Evans Brothers Limited
2A Portman Mansions
Chiltern Street
London W1M 1LE

First published 1992

Printed in Hong Kong by Dah Hua Printing Co. Ltd.

ISBN 0 237 51272 6

Acknowledgements

Editorial: Catherine Chambers and Jean Coppendale
Design : Pylon Design Consultants
Production: Jenny Mulvanny

Diagrams: Data Design

For permission to reproduce copyright material the author and
publishers gratefully acknowledge the following:

Cover: Main photograph - Blue and gold macaw, South America -
John Chellman, Oxford Scientific Films; inset photograph - Fire-
bellied toad - Alex Kerstitch, Planet Earth Pictures
Title page: Hibernating harlequin bugs from Australia - David
Maitland, Planet Earth Pictures
Contents page: Clown fish resting on a sea anemone, Tahiti -
Lewis Trusty, Oxford Scientific Films
Page 6 - (top left) Gryniewicz, Ecoscene, (top right) Rod Williams,
Bruce Coleman Limited, (bottom) A. Kerstitch, Planet Earth
Pictures; page 7 - (top) Michael Fogden, Oxford Scientific Films,
(above) Stephen Dalton, NHPA, (left) Tony Tilford, Oxford
Scientific Films; page 8 - (top) Hubert Kranemann, Oxford
Scientific Films, (left) Jane Burton, Bruce Coleman Limited, (right)
Peter Steyn, Ardea London Ltd; page 9 - (left) Warren Faidley,
Oxford Scientific Films, (right) Cooper, Ecoscene; page 10 - Felix
Labhardt, Bruce Coleman Limited; page 11 - Sally Morgan,
Ecoscene; page 12 - (top left) Rod Williams, Bruce Coleman
Limited, (top right) Hans Reinhard, Bruce Coleman Limited,
(bottom) Jane Burton, Bruce Coleman Limited; page 13 - C.B. &
D.W. Frith, Bruce Coleman Limited; page 14 - (left) Harold Taylor,
Oxford Scientific Films, (right) Jack A. Bailey, Ardea London Ltd;
page 15 - (top) Michael Freeman, Bruce Coleman Limited,
(bottom) Gryniewicz, Ecoscene; page 16 - (top) Hans Reinhard,
Bruce Coleman Limited, (above) Cooper, Ecoscene, (right)
Stephen Dalton, NHPA; page 17 - (top) J.P. Ferrero, Ardea
London Ltd, (bottom) Kjell Sandved, Oxford Scientific Films; page
18 - (top) K.G. Vock, Oxford Scientific Films, (above) P.L.
Fogden, Bruce Coleman Limited, (right) B & C Calhoun, Bruce
Coleman Limited; page 19 - (top) Robin Williams, Ecoscene, (left)
Zig Leszczynski, Oxford Scientific Films, (right) M.P.L. Fogden,
Bruce Coleman Limited; page 20 - (top) Greenwood, Ecoscene,
(bottom) Richard Kolar, Oxford Scientific Films; page 21 - (top)
Zig Leszczynski, Oxford Scientific Films, (bottom) Phil Devries,
Oxford Scientific Films; page 22 - (top) Sally Morgan, Ecoscene,
(above) Gryniewicz, Ecoscene, (bottom) David Purslow, Ecoscene;
page 23 - (top) Anthony Cooper, Ecoscene; (bottom) Sally Morgan,
Ecoscene; page 24 - (top) Oxford Scientific Films, (above) Sally
Morgan, Ecoscene, (bottom) Sally Morgan, Ecoscene; page 25 -
(top) Carl Roessler, Oxford Scientific Films, (top left) Anup Shah,
Planet Earth Pictures, (top right) Sally Morgan, Ecoscene, (bottom
left) Sally Morgan, Ecoscene, (bottom right) Ecoscene; page 26 -
(top) John Gerlach, Oxford Scientific Films, (bottom) Ron &
Valerie Taylor, Ardea London Ltd; page 27 -Towse, Ecoscene; page
28 - (top) Pat Morris, Ardea London Ltd, (above) Steven Kaufman,
Bruce Coleman Limited, (right) Eric Dragesco, Ardea London Ltd;
page 29 - (top) RAE, Ecoscene, (bottom) Sally Morgan, Ecoscene;
page 30 - (right) Hans Reinhard, Bruce Coleman Limited, (left)
Brian Coates, Bruce Coleman Limited; page 31 - (top) Philippa
Scott, NHPA, (bottom) Alan G. Nelson, Oxford Scientific Films;
page 32 - (top) David Thompson, Oxford Scientific Films, (bottom)
Wilhelm Moller, Ardea London Ltd; page 33 - (top) David & Katie
Urry, Ardea London Ltd, (bottom) David Purslow, Ecoscene; page
34 - W.E. Townsend jr, Bruce Coleman Limited; page 35 - (top)
Laurence Gould, Oxford Scientific Films, (bottom) Nicholls,
Ecoscene; page 36 - (top left) Leonard Lee Rue III, Oxford
Scientific Films, (top right) Gerald Cubitt, Bruce Coleman Limited,
(bottom right) Jim Clare, Oxford Scientific Films, (bottom left) Rod
Williams, Bruce Coleman Limited; page 37 - (top) Babs & Bert
Wells, Oxford Scientific Films, (bottom) J.M. Labat, Ardea London
Ltd; page 38 - (top) Silvestris, FLPA, (bottom) Pam & Willy Kemp,
Oxford Scientific Films; page 39 - (top) Herwarth Voigtmann,
Planet Earth Pictures, (bottom) David George, Planet Earth
Pictures; page 40 - (top) Ivan Polurich, NHPA, (left) Peter A.
Hinchcliffe, Bruce Coleman Limited, (right) Raymond Blythe,
Oxford Scientific Films; page 41 Peter David, Planet Earth Pictures;
page 43 - (top) Roland Mayr, Oxford Scientific Films, (bottom)
Jane Burton, Bruce Coleman Limited; page 44 - Jane Burton, Bruce
Coleman Limited; page 45 - (top) Eric Crichton, Bruce Coleman
Limited, (above) Eric Crichton, Bruce Coleman Limited, (bottom)
Michael P. Price, Bruce Coleman Limited

Contents

Introduction

In this book we are going to look at animals and colour. We will discover how animals see colour, and find out why colour is so important to them.

Above left: Some animals, like the giraffe, use their spots to blend in with patches of sunlight under trees

Above right: Male splendid fairy or blue wren in its bright breeding plumage

Right: The bright red stripes of this lion fish warn others that it is dangerous

Top: The Australian frilled lizard opens a huge frill around its neck when it is attacked. The size and colour of the frill are usually enough to scare away the attacker

Above: The dark brown and yellow spots of the spotted salamander have an important message for predators

Left: The brightly coloured feathers of the red lory are easy to spot by an interested mate

How animals see colour

The blue pigments of this feather reflect some colours and absorb others

Without light there can be no colour. The beautiful plumage of peacocks, the **iridescent** scales of tropical fish and the red breast of the robin all would be colourless without light.

All around us we can see everyday things – the chairs and tables in the room in which we sit, and the trees and cars outside. These objects do not have or produce their own light. So how can we see them? They are **reflecting** the light that falls on them; the daylight from the sun, and at night the light from lamps or a fire, or the moonlight.

Light is reflected off all objects and it travels in straight lines. Because these objects reflect light in straight lines, we can see their true shape. We can also see their colour.

Above: During daylight it is possible to see the shape of the animal and the colour of its fur, but the bush-baby is very sensitive to bright light and seems shy

Left: This bush-baby is very difficult to see at night. Only the light reflected from the back of its beautiful big eyes can be seen

The feathers of the chest of this robin reflect red light, so we see a red breast. Robins are small but they are very fierce birds

Some of the colours of the spectrum can be seen clearly in this rainbow, with red on one side, blue on the other and green in the middle

The skin, fur, feathers or shells of almost all animals in the world contain **pigments** which appear coloured. This is because they reflect just some of the colours of the light which falls on them, and **absorb** the rest. When colours are absorbed they do not bounce back for us to see them. So a robin's breast looks red because only red light is reflected from it. The other colours are absorbed. The moon does not produce any light at all, but reflects the light from the sun. Without the sun, we would not see the moon.

The sun gives off light that we can see. It is called visible light. But it also gives off two kinds of light which we cannot see: ultra-violet and infra-red. Although we cannot see infra-red light, we can feel it as heat. Some cameras loaded with special film can **detect** infra-red light and can take pictures in the dark. Our skins can detect ultra-violet – it is the light that changes the colour in pale skin and gives it a suntan.

Sunlight, or white light, is really a mixture of colours which we call a spectrum. The colours of the spectrum are red, orange, yellow, green, blue, indigo and violet, in that order.

COLOURFUL WORDS!

iridescent: shiny, silvery rainbow colours
reflecting: bouncing off something
pigment: the natural colouring of something, or something which gives a colour
absorb: to soak up something
detect: to find or discover

9

What do animals see ?

Almost all animals can react to light in some way, but not all have eyes like ourselves. The earthworm has no eyes. Instead it has skin that is **sensitive** to light. In fact the earthworm dies quickly if left exposed to ultra-violet light for even just an hour or so. This sensitivity to light allows the worm to know when it is safe to leave its burrow in the soil.

Most animals, however, do have eyes, but there are several different types. Some of these eyes are quite unlike our own. Although the various types of eye are constructed differently, they have one thing in common – they all see by detecting and collecting light. They are just like miniature cameras.

Insects have very **complex** eyes. Each eye is actually made of many tiny lenses, packed very closely together. It is called a compound eye. If you were to look through an insect's eye, it would be like looking through many eyes at the same time, each giving its own picture of the world.

Animals with backbones are called vertebrates. Humans are vertebrates, and so are fish, amphibians such as frogs, reptiles such as snakes and birds. They have a very different kind of eye: one with a single lens in the front.

The vertebrate eye is rather like a ping-pong ball with a clear window on one side – the lens. Eyes are filled with what looks like a clear jelly. This jelly-like substance lets the light through but keeps the eye the right shape. The eye is connected to the brain by a nerve – the optic nerve. This is a small white cord that runs from the back of the eye to the brain. It takes messages from one to the other.

A lens is used to **focus** the light reflected from an object. The brain works out that this sharp **image** is the object that the eye focused on.

In front of the lens is the iris, which opens and closes like a curtain to control the amount of light that enters the eye. The iris is important, because too much light entering the eye can cause damage. It is coloured, and in humans it can be blue, green, grey or brown. In the middle of the iris is a black hole, called the pupil, which lets light through to the back of the eye.

The huge eyes of this dragonfly, a type of insect, are actually made up of 10,000 tiny lenses packed together to form a compound eye

The inside of the eye is covered with a coating of special **cells** which are sensitive to light. This coating is called the retina. When light hits the cells of the retina they start to react, and a message is sent to the brain. The retina contains thousands of cells. There are two kinds of cell in the retina – the rods which enable us to see in black and white, and the cones which enable us to see colour when there is bright light. There are three types of cone – one for detecting blue, one for green and the third for red. They work together to enable us to see all the colours of the spectrum.

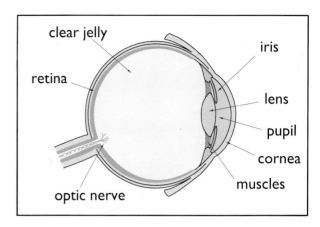

A diagram of a vertebrate's eye

COLOURFUL THINGS TO DO

Field of vision

This experiment tests what you see to the sides of where you are actually looking. This is called peripheral vision. You may not notice it all the time, but if you look straight at something, you are still aware of other objects lying to one side or the other. But can you tell what colour these other objects are without looking directly at them?

1 You will need four pairs of coloured cards at least 10 cm square (10 cm long and 10 cm wide), and a partner. Each pair of cards should be a different colour.

2 One person sits on a chair and the other person stands behind it.

3 The person behind holds the cards, one in each hand, out to the side of the person sitting down, starting behind the level of their ear.

4 The cards are then slowly brought forward.

5 The person sitting down has to say when they can see the cards, and what colour they are. This is then tried with the other colours.

The distance between the points on either side of your head where you first saw the cards, is called your field of vision.

How wide is your field of vision?

Which colours can you see best at the edge of your vision?

Why are emergency vehicles such as fire-engines painted bright colours?

What do animals see?

If you look carefully at the eyes in the two pictures of this eagle owl you will see a difference. In one the pupil is a very small circle in the middle of the eye. In the other the pupil is much larger. The size of the pupil changes as the light levels change. In bright light the pupil will be small to stop too much light getting into the eye and damaging it

This white flower is not really white to the bumble bee who is collecting the pollen. She sees it as a dazzling ultra-violet beacon. It acts as a powerful signal, leading the bee towards the pollen or nectar

When you have been out of doors at night, have you ever noticed that you can only see in black and white? If you leave a brightly lit house, in which you see everything in colour, at first you cannot see anything. After a few minutes, as your eyes become used to the low light level, you start to see things. But they are only in black and white. This is because the cones, which can detect colour, can only work in bright light. The rods work well in dim light because they are more sensitive. But they can only see black and white.

Most animals have cells in their eyes which respond to visible light, that is, light that can be seen. But some animals have specially adapted eyes which can detect infra-red or ultra-violet light. These kinds of light are often called IR or UV for short. Goldfish, for example, can see IR light.

Bees, on the other hand, cannot see red or orange. But they can see the visible spectrum from yellow to violet, and beyond it, into the UV region. This means that they can see colours which humans cannot see. A flower which looks drab to us can be colourful to a bee. UV colours are the brightest and most **luminous** seen by bees.

Colour in Animals

Some snakes, such as the pit viper, have special **organs** for detecting IR **radiation**. These organs help the snake to find its prey, that is, the animals which it feeds on. The bodies of these animals give off heat, which the snake's special organs detect as IR radiation.

At night the pit viper can see its prey, but the prey cannot see the pit viper

COLOURFUL THINGS TO DO

The bee's favourite colour

In this project you are going to find out which colours bees prefer. Bees are only active in the summer, so you should try this out on a warm, sunny day.

1 Cut out circles of different coloured card, e.g. blue, red, white, pink.

2 Place them outside in an open position.

3 Put some sugary water on a small dish such as a small saucer or petri dish and place it on the centre of each card.

4 Wait for the bees to find the cards. Which one do they go to first? Do they like one card, or some, more than others? In other words, do they have a preference?

You could repeat the test by just having sugary water on one card.

Watch the flowers in your garden. Do bees seem to prefer any particular flowers?

honey bee feeding on sugary water

sugary water

coloured card

dish

Why do animals look coloured ?

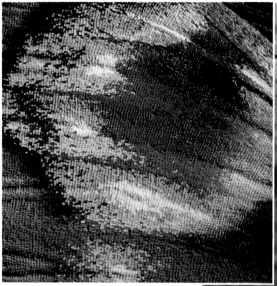

Above: The tiny scales of the peacock butterfly's wings look like a beautiful sewn tapestry

Right: The colours of the peacock butterfly's wings are produced by the refection of light

The colour of an animal is produced in one of two different ways, or by both together. Many animals look coloured because they reflect certain colours of light off their bodies. Others have coloured pigments on their scales, skin or fur which absorb some colours and not others.

Fur, feathers and scales can all reflect colour. Insects such as butterflies and moths often have beautifully coloured, iridescent wings. Most of these colours are produced by tiny scales which cover the wings. Very small grooves and ridges cross the surface of these scales. The grooves and ridges cause light to be reflected in special patterns which form bands of colour. You can get the same result if you hold a compact disc up to the light at an angle. What happens to the colours as you change the angle of the disc? The same thing happens if you look at a butterfly from a different angle.

Other animals produce colour from pigments. Various parts of the body can be coloured in this way. The iris of the human eye gets its brown, green, grey or blue colour from a pigment. What colour are your eyes?

Other parts of the body can be coloured, such as the skin. Skin contains a special pigment called melanin, which causes it to look brown. For peoples with dark brown skin who live in hot sunny climates, the pigment is important because it can protect their skin from the harmful UV radiation given off by the sun. These peoples also have brown eyes which are less sensitive to the strong, harmful sunlight.

In cooler areas of the world where there is less sun, protection from it is not so important. So these peoples have paler skin with less pigment. Although some of them have brown eyes, others have blue, green or grey eyes, which are more sensitive to light. However, if people with pale skin sit in the sun, the melanin in their skin can turn brown, producing a tan. Sometimes, though, it can turn red and burn !

Pigments are also found in hair, fur, feathers, scales and shells. The hair of humans comes in several colours. The most common colours are brown, black, blond and red. What other hair colours do mammals have?

The body of a bird is covered in feathers. It is the feathers that give the bird its colour. Feathers are made of a tough material called keratin. There are several types of feather and they all have different jobs to do.

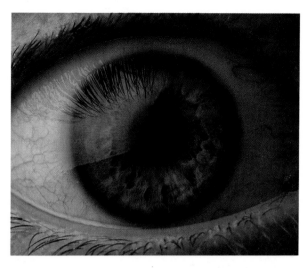

The colour of this eye is produced by a blue pigment in the cells of the iris

The dark skin of this Maasai warrior is perfect protection against the strong African sun

15

Why do animals look coloured ?

The smaller feathers are fluffy, and are found close to the skin of the bird. They are used to trap pockets of air and this stops body heat from escaping. The feathers therefore act as insulation or protection against the cold. These feathers are called 'down'. The largest feathers are firm and flexible and are used for flight. They are made of many tiny strands of fibre-like threads, which are attached to a shaft in the centre. Each strand has hundreds of tiny barbs which hook into each other so that they hold the strands together.

The beautiful colours of the hummingbird, kingfisher and peacock are produced by light reflecting from the oils which cover their feathers. However, even colourful birds look quite drab in the rain. The spectacular blue-fronted macaw from the Amazon rainforest has lovely green feathers that turn a drab brown in the rain! This happens because wet feathers cannot reflect light properly.

Top: Compare the colours of this Himalayan monal pheasant with those of the kingfisher below

Above: A few animals get their colour from the plants or animals which they eat. The pretty pink of the flamingo comes from the colour of the tiny water creatures which it eats. In zoos, where these very small animals cannot be obtained, the flamingo's food has to be dyed pink to keep the birds looking their natural colour

As the kingfisher flies, the oils in its bright feathers catch and reflect light giving them a shimmering appearance

Colour in Animals

The white and yellow colours of butterflies often come from chemicals in the plants which they ate when they were caterpillars.

Often the bright colours of an animal fade with age. The scales of a butterfly's wing may drop out, so the butterfly loses its shimmering appearance. However, some animals have ways of getting back their beautiful colours. Reptiles such as snakes and lizards at certain times shed their entire skin as they grow, revealing a new and brighter skin beneath. The feathers of birds become rough and worn, so twice a year the old feathers are replaced with new ones which are bright and fresh.

The old skin of this snake is thin and worn and the colours have faded. But the skin underneath has bright, undamaged scales

COLOURFUL THINGS TO DO

Feathers

Feathers come in all colours and shapes. Collect some feathers and examine them in a good light. Peacock or pheasant feathers are particularly colourful. Where is the colour?

Look at your feathers with a hand lens. Can you see the barbs and little hooks that hold the feathers together?

Warning colours

Many animals are brightly coloured because they want to attract attention to themselves – they want to be seen. Their colour means **DANGER**. It is a warning to a hungry **predator** that it would be dangerous to try to eat them. This is because they can be poisonous.

A common warning developed by many animals is a pattern of yellow and black stripes. The wasp is a good example of this. Even though only female wasps sting, male wasps have the same colours. Predators cannot tell the difference between male and female. They avoid them both.

Many amphibians, animals such as toads, frogs and newts, are poisonous. They also have warning colours. The slow-moving spotted salamander seems an easy target for a hungry predator. But it has a dark brown body with yellow spots (see photograph on page 7). This is a warning that the salamander has poison glands in its skin which would make a predator sick if it ate it. The salamander has similar colours to the wasp. Dark brown and yellow make a very clear signal to a predator.

Skunks have black-and-white markings on their body and tail. Although not actually poisonous, they can spray an attacker with an incredibly foul smelling liquid. The smell is almost impossible to wash off, and lasts for many days. If attacked, skunks wave their black-and-white tails in warning. Only if this is ignored will the skunk use its smelly spray. This warning, and the horrible result of ignoring it, has been so successful that no animal hunts the skunk.

Top: The yellow-and-black stripes of the wasp are a clear warning that it might have a painful sting

Above: The poison-arrow frogs from the rainforests of South America have spectacular colours. The bright pinks, yellows and blues advertise the fact that the frogs are very poisonous. Their skin produces a **toxin** that is so poisonous that the tiniest amount can kill a man

Right: No human or animal would want to go near a skunk waving its tail in the air

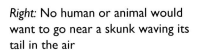

The caterpillars of many moths and butterflies feed on poisonous plants. They take in the plant's poison and so become poisonous themselves. The caterpillar of the cinnabar moth feeds on ragwort. This plant contains a poison that will make other animals ill. The caterpillar is coloured yellow and black as a warning. Some are still poisonous even after they have changed into moths.

Some animals hide their warning colours until they are threatened. Then, they will suddenly produce a brightly coloured wing or patch. The peacock butterfly rests with its wings held above its body. But if a predator, such as bird, appears the butterfly will lower its wings to reveal large eyespots. These eyespots are vividly coloured in yellow, black and red, and are designed to scare away any predator. The peacock butterfly may even open and close its wings several times to draw attention to the eye spot.

The Australian frilled lizard has several hidden messages. When it is attacked, it first opens a huge frill around its neck, see page 7. This is decorated in black, white and yellow spots. Both the size and colour of the frill are usually enough to scare away the attacker. But if necessary it can also open its mouth to show a bright yellow lining. This is another danger signal!

Using colours as a warning can only work if predators learn to avoid particular animals. Poisonous animals have bright, contrasting colours and bold shapes so that they are as easy as possible to recognize. A predator might eat one animal by mistake, but will be sick, and will learn to avoid that animal's colours in the future. Although this is too late for the animal that was eaten, it will help others like it to survive.

The pattern and colours of this cinnabar caterpillar warn predators not to eat it

COLOURFUL WORDS!

predator: an animal which hunts, kills and eats another animal, or prey

toxin: poison

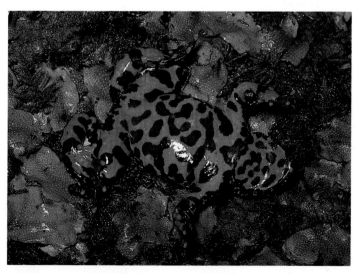

The fire-bellied toad has a green-and-black spotted skin which blends in well with green plants. But when it is threatened, it flips on to its back to reveal a bright red-and-black belly. These fiery colours are a strong warning!

Copy-cats

The hoverfly is a very good mimic. Compare this picture of a hoverfly with that of the wasp on page 18. Can you spot the differences? Would you be fooled by the mimicry?

There are many animals that look as if they are poisonous but in fact are quite tasty. They are copying the colours of animals that are poisonous so that they, too, do not get eaten. This is called mimicry.

There are good examples of mimicry in some of the more common insects. The yellow-and-black colourings of the wasp that does have a poisonous sting, are copied by the hoverfly. At first glance the hoverfly looks just like a wasp. It is yellow and black, but it has only one pair of wings instead of two. But it does not have the sting and narrow waist that the wasp has.

The wasp is a popular animal to copy. For example, the clear-wing moth also looks like the wasp. One South African cricket has gone to extraordinary lengths to copy a wasp. It not only has the same colouring, but also mimics the wasp's shape. This cricket only walks on five of its six legs. The sixth leg is held out behind the body to look like the wasp's sting!

Would you mistake this caterpillar for a snake?

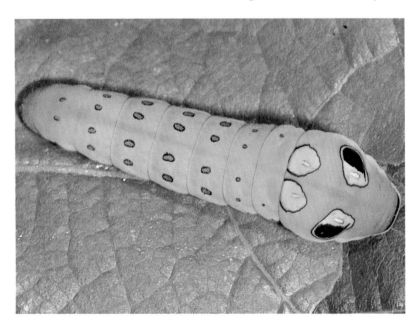

A caterpillar in the rainforests of Central America can be mistaken for a snake. Its tail end is shaped like the head of the viper! There are also many attractive swallowtail butterflies living in the tropical rainforests. Only two of the swallowtail **species** are poisonous but none of the others are. They simply mimic the appearance of the two poisonous types.

The hairstreak butterfly actually mimics itself to deceive a predator. The bottom of its wings have, over the ages, **evolved** to look like its own antennae. As the wings move, these false antennae move around just like the real ones. Predatory birds are deceived into pecking at the false head, leaving the real head alone.

However good the mimic is, mimicry only works if the predator eats the genuinely poisonous animals more than the mimic. This means that the original and the mimic must live in the same **habitat**. If they do not, the warning signal copied by the mimic will become meaningless.

Look at this copperhead snake wiggling its yellow tail in such a way that the frog thinks it is a worm! When the frog gets close enough, the snake will strike

This hairstreak butterfly looks as if it has two heads but one is false. Which is the false head?

21

Hiding in plain sight

The zebra's stripes look very sharp and bright on the open plains, but they are good camouflage amongst trees and tall grass

Birds would not see this buff-tip moth because it looks just like a twig

Almost every animal is the prey of some other animal. But if the hunter cannot see its prey, it cannot catch and eat it. By using its colours and patterns to fit in with its background, an animal can seem to disappear. This is called camouflage.

Some animals, like the giraffe, use their spots to blend in with patches of sunlight under trees. It is difficult to see a zebra's stripes in the long grass of the African plains, especially in the late afternoon when there are long shadows. At this time of day these animals are at greatest risk from their predators, lions. Although this type of camouflage works well from a distance, the size and shape of the zebra and the giraffe are hard to disguise when they are not far away.

Some animals have developed camouflage so well that they become almost totally invisible, even when seen close up. Some insects have wings which are perfect copies of tree bark, leaves or even thorns and flowers. They have evolved their special shape and colour over many thousands of years.

Some birds rely on camouflage to hide their eggs. The ringed plover lays its eggs on pebbly beaches. It does not make a nest, but the spotted eggs are almost impossible to see amongst the small stones.

This common lizard blends perfectly with its background of dead twigs and leaves

The ringed plover lays its eggs amongst pebbles. How many spotted eggs can you see in this picture?

COLOURFUL THINGS TO DO

Disappearing act

A good way to keep hidden is simply to stay still. This simple project shows how much better camouflage can be if an animal stays still.

1 You will need two pieces of black paper about 20 cm wide and 20 cm long, a small amount of thick white paint, a paintbrush and a piece of clear plastic the same size as the paper.

2 Cut out an animal's shape from one piece of paper. Leave a long piece of paper to act as a handle. Use the paint to make a **random** pattern of white dots on the paper.

3 Make some more random dots all over the second piece of paper. This will act as a background for the animal.

4 Place the cut-out animal on the background and cover both pieces of paper with the plastic. This keeps the cut-out animal flat against the background.

5 Stand a metre away from the paper. Can you see the shape of the animal? If you can, just move back another metre. Now place the cut-out so that you can move the animal by the handle while it is still under the plastic. Can you see it now?

You could do this with friends and cut out several different animal shapes. See if anyone can identify the animal before it is moved. Who can identify it first when it is moved?

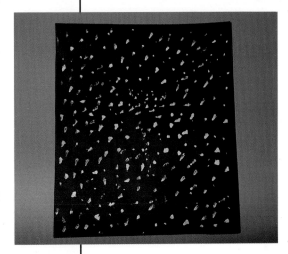

Lying in wait

Camouflage is very useful for animals trying to avoid predators. But it is just as useful for predators wanting to get close to their prey before striking.

Some of the big cats such as the tiger, jaguar and leopard have spotted or striped coats. This breaks up their solid shape so that they can hide themselves in the vegetation where they hunt. The lion can hide itself in grassland even though its coat has no pattern. The golden colour of its fur blends perfectly with the long, dry grass of the African plains. When hunting, the big cats move especially slowly, so that their movement does

not warn their prey. If they think that the prey might be about to spot them, the cats freeze like a statue.

One species of praying mantis found in the rainforests of Malaysia lives amongst the white petals of an orchid. Its legs are shaped just like petals. While it is still, it is almost impossible to spot. If an insect lands on the flower, however, the mantis shoots out its arms and catches it!

The British crab spider has exactly the same tactics. Its colour matches that of the flower on which it waits for small

Top: This flower mantis is waiting to pounce on an insect looking for pollen and nectar

Above: This lioness is perfectly camouflaged in the long grass of the African plains. It is very difficult for other animals to see her quietly creeping up on its prey

The crab spider has successfully caught this bee that landed on the spotted orchid looking for nectar

insects. When the insect, perhaps a bee, lands on the flower to collect **pollen** and **nectar**, it is caught by the spider. The spider then injects a poison into it. The poison **paralyzes** the bee, which is eaten later.

One of the most dangerous animals of **tropical** seas is the stone-fish. It is a master of camouflage. Perfectly matching the surrounding rocks, it is almost invisible to the eye. If a diver is unlucky enough to tread on a stone-fish, he will usually get a poisonous sting which attacks the muscles. If not treated, a person stung by the fish can die within just a few hours.

The spines and growths on the body of this pink stone-fish make it look just like the rocks all around it while its skin changes colour to suit the new background

COLOURFUL THINGS TO DO

Spot the tiger

1 Trace the tiger onto a sheet of paper.
2 Colour it in with yellow and brown crayons.
3 Carefully cut it out.
4 Place it against each background in turn.
Where is the best place for the tiger to hunt?
What type of animal would hunt in the other places?

COLOURFUL WORDS!

pollen: yellow dust inside flowers which helps to make seeds

nectar: the sugary water made inside the flower

paralyzes: stops something from being able to move

tropical: the hot part of the world between the two tropics: Cancer and Capricorn

Changing colour

So far, we have seen how well camouflage can work when an animal remains very still, and how a little movement can make an animal much easier to spot. Of course, almost all animals have to move at some time in order to search for food. When an animal moves from one type of **cover** to another, it is more likely to be seen by a predator, or be noticed by its prey.

In addition, the animal may move from an area where it fits in well with the surroundings, to an area where it is less well camouflaged. For example, a brown moth lying in the dappled sunlight on the trunk of a tree will be seen much more easily if it takes off and accidentally lands on a bright green leaf.

Most animals learn to avoid showing themselves against a background which does not match their own colour and

This chameleon is green, to blend with the green leaves on the twig

pattern. But some have developed the ability to actually change their own colour to match their surroundings.

The master of this colour change is the chameleon. Sitting on a leafy branch, the chameleon will be green. But if it moves onto one with less leaves and more branch, it will change its colour over a quarter of an hour, to a brown shade to match the colour of the branches.

Scientists have found out that not only the eyes, but also parts of the chameleon's skin, can detect and measure colour. When a chameleon needs to change colour, messages are sent to the brain, and the brain tells the skin to change colour. It does this in a very simple way.

Pigments are contained in four separate layers within the chameleon's scaly skin. Each layer contains a different pigment; black, blue, white or yellow. The size of the cells in each layer can be controlled by signals from the brain. By **combining** sizes of pigment cells in different ways, and therefore the 'mixture' of reflected light, the chameleon is able to change its colour.

Chameleons are not the only animals which can do this. Many flat-fish can match the colours and patterns of the sea bed on which they lie. Their skin mimics whatever their eyes see, often so well that they become almost totally invisible.

The plaice has a spotted skin, which makes it easier for the fish to blend in with the colours of the sea bed on which it lies

COLOURFUL WORDS!

cover: something that prey or predator can hide behind, such as trees, bushes or grass

combining: using together

Seasonal changes in colour

In some parts of the world, especially the colder areas, the landscape changes with the season. The land is green and brown in summer but is changed into a landscape of white in winter. Animals that are well camouflaged in brown and green habitats become very easy to see against the snow. Some animals solve this problem by changing the colour of their coat.

The arctic hare grows a special winter coat which is white, to help it stay hidden from eagles when it moves around on the snow. In the spring, as the snow melts, it sheds its white coat and grows a brown summer one. This is a good camouflage against the grass covered hillsides.

The colour change does not happen instantly but over a number of weeks as the old hairs fall out and are replaced by new ones. So, for a number of weeks, it has a rather mottled brown-and-white appearance.

The rock ptarmigan lives in the mountains of the far north, and right up into the cold arctic regions of the world. It feeds on small arctic plants but in turn is preyed upon by eagles and foxes. In the summer, the bird has a mottled brown plumage to blend in with the rocks and **lichens,** but in winter its plumage has to change because snow lies on the ground. In autumn, its

The arctic hare looks like an ordinary hare in the summer. It only looks different in winter when it has a white coat to blend with the snow

The rock ptarmigan's white winter feathers gradually fall out in spring and are replaced with dark ones

feathers begin to change to a pure white so that the ptarmigan can blend with the winter snow. In spring, the male ptarmigan does not lose its winter colour as quickly as the female. It keeps its white coat for a number of weeks while the female is on the nest. It is thought that the more obvious colour of the male attracts predators and so draws attention away from the female and the young.

The polar bear has a thick white fur for camouflage, but underneath has a black skin

COLOURFUL THINGS TO DO

Black or white

Polar bears have a thick white coat which is ideal camouflage for living in the Arctic. However, the skin beneath this white coat is black. In this project you will discover why this is important.

1 You will need two jars: one painted white, the other black, both with lids. Punch holes in the middle of the lids. You will also need two thermometers.

2 Fill both jars with water, replace the lids and push the thermometers through the hole in the middle of each lid.

3 Make a note of the temperature of the water in each jar.

4 Now place both jars in front of a radiator, a fan heater, or on a sunny window ledge. How quickly does the temperature in each jar rise?

Is there any difference?

Why should this be important for the polar bear?

Why do we wear white clothes in summer?

Courtship colours

Look at the bird-of-paradise hanging up-side-down from a branch. He does not look much like the one standing the right way up!

Colour is a particularly important part of **courtship** in many animals. Many males make use of great displays of colour to attract a possible female as a mate. Some animals shed their drab camouflage colours in the breeding season and produce a new brightly-coloured outfit. Sometimes these new feathers come complete with crests and plumes to make the animal even more attractive.

In most species of duck there are differences between the colours of males and females. The males, or drakes, have brightly-coloured feathers. The female's feathers are drab and **inconspicuous** so that she will be well hidden when she is on the nest. Courtship usually takes place in spring before nesting gets underway. The displays help to make a bond between the male and female so that they stay together.

Once a male and female have paired, they build a nest and the female lays eggs. However, for a short period while the pair are rearing their young, the male loses his beautiful feathers and he also looks drab. This makes the male duck harder for predators to see while he is on or near the nest.

The bright colours of the male help it to attract a mate, while the dull plumage of the female acts as camouflage, for she spends a lot of time either on the nest or looking after the young ducklings.

One of the most spectacular displays of courtship colour is produced by the peacock. A peacock has three types of feather in his fan. Near the edge the feathers are short and curved forming an attractive fringe. The main feathers are large, with eye patterns. They end in fish-tails.

The male bird-of-paradise, a bird of the forest, has also developed a colourful and strange courtship dance involving colour, shape and even acrobatics! He has brightly coloured wings and feathers that sprout from his legs and lower breast.

During courtship displays he grips a branch, topples backwards and hangs upside-down. He then spreads his feathers into a brilliantly coloured fan. As he does this, long quills twice the length of his body, are waved about him, to end a display rich enough to attract any female watching. The long, special courting feathers make moving around the forest difficult, so at the end of the breeding season these feathers fall out.

The male mandarin duck has feathers of green, orange and brown, with a ruff of pointed feathers around his neck and a strange sail sprouting from his wings. This drake then shows off in front of the female duck, dipping his beak in the water, arching his neck and opening the sail on his wing, just like a fan, while making bubbling sounds

COLOURFUL WORDS!

courtship: trying to attract a mate

inconspicuous: something that does not show up well enough to catch the eye

elaborate: complicated

pulsated: beats like a heart

The male peacock uses his huge fan of feathers to attract a female. It seems that as a male gets older he gains more of each type of feather in his fan. His fan is an advert. A large fan is a sign to the female that he is healthy and fit to be a father

The importance of red

This male stickleback has attracted a female with its red belly. Here you can see him leading her to the opening of the nest that he has built from pondweed

Red is a very important courtship signal for frigate birds. Frigate birds spend most of their lives at sea, and only come ashore to build a nest and rear their young. Once the male has found a good place for a nest, he inflates his huge scarlet throat pouch with air as an invitation for the female to come and join him

Red is a colour which is of special importance to some animals. A well-known example is the robin, which is highly aggressive when it is defending its territory. It thrusts its red breast towards an enemy as a signal that it is about to attack.

The male stickleback is a small fish which develops a red belly during the breeding season. He takes an area of pond which he thinks of as his own. He then builds a tunnel of small plants into which he attracts the female to lay her eggs. She is drawn to the red belly of the male stickleback. But if he sees the red belly of another male in his territory he will attack it. The red signal is so strong that he will attack anything red, even if it is not alive, such as a piece of wax.

Newly-hatched herring-gull chicks also act on the colour red. As soon as they are born, they peck upward towards the female's bill, and the adult responds by giving them food. Although the bill is mostly yellow, it has a large red spot at the end. This **programmed behaviour** is so strong that young chicks will stab at anything red, even cherries.

Dunnocks have no red spot on the bill, but the whole of the inside of the chick's mouth is bright red, making a good target for the mother bird.

Many chicks, like these dunnocks, open their bills to reveal a bright red mouth when the female arrives at the nest with food. The red mouth is a signal to make the female feed them

Herring-gull chicks know that they must peck at the red spot at the end of the mother's bill to make her feed them

COLOURFUL WORDS!

programmed behaviour: something an animal will do automatically, without thinking

Bright colours in tropical waters

Tropical seas contain many examples of brightly coloured animals. Bright colours are found particularly amongst the complex and beautiful coral reefs.

Reefs are found only in warm coastal waters, where the temperature is at least 19°C and the water depth is less than 90 metres. The size of a reef can range from just a few metres long to many thousands of kilometres. The Australian Great Barrier Reef is over 3,200 kilometres long. It is the largest structure made by animals.

Corals may look like plants but they are actually tiny animals related to sea anemones. They have soft bodies and tentacles, and rely for protection on a hard case made of limestone which they build around themselves.

Corals live in colonies of many thousands of the same kind. As the colony grows, more skeleton is laid down and so the size of the coral colony increases. As each coral grows, so the whole reef of different corals gets larger.

Corals come in many colours. Some of the most spectacular corals to be found anywhere in the world are the red corals of the Mediterranean. The limestone skeleton is actually pigmented. The ancient Romans used this beautiful red coral as jewellery. Coral forms the basis of the whole reef. Animals live in and around the coral. Some even eat the coral itself.

Not only are the corals colourful, but so are many of the tropical fish which live in them. Fish which inhabit tropical seas have far brighter colours than those fish which live in cooler seas. Why is this so?

Well, there are many more fish in warmer waters than in cooler ones. In these crowded conditions it may be necessary to use bright colours to help identify other fish of the same kind, and to attract a mate. Also, warmer waters are clearer. So visual signals such as bright colours are more effective.

Although the clown fish is not poisonous itself, its colours are a warning that it lives in a sea anemone that is poisonous

The colour of fish is produced by pigment-filled cells in the skin. These pigments are often very bright, with some cells making iridescent colours, just like those found when oil forms a film on water.

The colours of many tropical fish are warnings. The lion fish with its striped body advertizes the fact that it has poisonous spines (see page 6). Clown fish actually live amongst the poisonous tentacles of a sea anemone, but they are **immune** to its poison. Other fish do not have immunity. So the colours of the clown fish signal a warning that it would be dangerous to try to eat it.

Top: Reefs are very colourful habitats, with corals and fish of every imaginable colour

Above: Look quickly at this picture. Could you see the shape of the fish straight away?

Surprisingly, some of the brightest fish are well camouflaged. The bold patterns of bright colours actually help to disguise the shape of the fish against the corals. It is very difficult to work out what shape the fish really is. This type of camouflage is called disruptive colouration.

When it is dark, and colours cannot be seen, it is not useful to be brightly coloured. Divers have noticed that brightly coloured fish actually fade at night, until it is almost impossible to recognize them! However, all it takes to make the bright colour come back is to shine a torch on them for a few seconds.

COLOURFUL WORDS!

immune: not harmed by a certain poison or disease

Bright colours in the rainforest

The hornbills that live in rainforests are much bigger and more colourful than those hornbills that live in grasslands. In the dark rainforest they have to make themselves more easily visible

The rainforest is a dark place with twisted branches and huge tree trunks. The leaves of trees and bushes come in every shade of green imaginable. The shrill noises of animals calling is almost deafening at times. Heavy rains wash away any smells or scents. This, and the thick undergrowth, make it hard to see very far. So many animals are very brightly coloured to help draw attention to themselves and to attract a mate.

The uakari monkey has a brilliant red face that is a complementary colour to the green colours of the forest. It gives different signals to other monkeys in the forest

Many of the birds are brightly coloured and bigger than similar birds found elsewhere. For example, the hornbill of the rainforest is bigger and more colourful than its **savanna** cousin.

A common colour in the rainforest is red, which is a **complementary colour** to green. Many birds have green feathers with contrasting flashes of red. The flashing of the bright colour can have many different meanings. For a lorikeet it means 'keep away' but for the turaco it means 'follow me'!

The bower bird has an unusually strong liking for blue objects. It lives in the darker parts of the forest. But when the male is ready to attract a mate, he strips the leaves from the forest trees above his chosen courting area so that sunlight can reach the floor and strike his bright feathers and his collection of blue objects. Some bower birds collect coloured objects and make a display of their collection at either end of their nest, known as a bower. This collection helps them to attract a mate.

The male blue bower bird collects all sorts of blue objects and arranges them around his nest, or bower, to impress a female. He will even steal them

The toucan has a huge brightly-coloured bill that stands out in the green forest. The bill is very strong, so it is ideal for breaking nuts

COLOURFUL WORDS!

savanna: dry grassland with low bushes and few trees
complementary colour: the 'opposite' colour, one which contrasts strongly

Communicating with colour

In humans, a red face is usually brought about by either anger or embarrassment. It acts as a signal to other people, whether we want it to or not! We are communicating what we feel through the use of colour. Similar use of colour is common amongst the rest of the animal kingdom.

Octopus and squid can change their body colours at will, to show emotion. An angry octopus will turn red, but it will turn white if scared. Some reef squid have a visual language. They actually appear to communicate by using colours and patterns on their bodies.

The secret is in their skins, where tiny cells are filled with different pigments. Each cell can be instructed by the squid's brain to get larger or smaller very quickly. This allows patterns of colour to sweep across its body. These patterns can be stripes, spots or blotches. The squid can move them in complex ways on the skin. So far, scientists have discovered more than 35 different types of pattern, but they do not yet know what they mean.

The male mandrill, a West African baboon, has a face with a ridged and furrowed, brightly-coloured mask which is shaped into a fake snarl. This grim face is a strong warning signal to his enemies in the dark undergrowth of the rainforest in which he lives

Look at the colour of this octopus. Is it angry or scared?

This pair of cuttlefish are sending messages to each other by changing the patterns of colours in their skin

Cuttlefish can do the same, and can even give out one message on one side of their bodies and another on the other side. For example, if a male cuttlefish is courting a female, and another male sneaks up behind him, the male in the middle will communicate one message to the female, but will send a very different one to the unwelcome male! The male intruder, as he is being warned away, will not even be able to see that the male in the middle is 'chatting up' the female.

One highly adapted rainforest frog lives only beside waterfalls. Because of the constant noise of the waterfall, he cannot use sound to attract a mate. Instead, these frogs have evolved bright blue feet, which they wave about to attract females.

The stripes of colour on the skin of this cuttlefish are also messages, but scientists are still trying to work out just what each pattern means

A light in the darkness

Thousands of male fire-flies, all flashing at the same time, can be seen over long distances

Animals which sleep during the day, and come out to feed at night, are called nocturnal. Many of them need to communicate in the dark. Some have developed an amazing ability to do this by using light which is made in the cells of their bodies.

Glow-worms and fireflies are the best known examples. They are not flies or worms at all, but are in fact species of night-flying beetle. Their bodies make a substance called luciferin. When luciferin is mixed with oxygen from the air, it gives these beetles their bright glow. The light is used to help them to see at night, and also to communicate with one another.

At night, in the mangrove swamps of Malaysia, many thousands of fireflies on the wing make an impressive sight. Their flashes are signals like Morse Code. But they are far more complex, with long and short bursts of light which are very difficult for the human eye to see.

The swamp fireflies gather on certain bushes and time their flashes so that eventually they all flash on and off together. These flashes can be seen over 400 metres away, making an unmistakable signal to any female fireflies in the area. The females cannot fail to know where to find a mate, since only the males flash.

The female glow worm produces an eerie glow from her abdomen. This glow is more easily seen at night

At certain times of the year, in the waters off Panama in South America, green spots of light flash on and off around fish and divers alike. This ghostly light is made by fire-fleas, which are small **crustaceans** like water-fleas. They produce a sudden green flash to scare away predators.

Fish which live in the deep, dark, cold waters of the ocean use light for hunting. They use lots of special **bacteria** which glow in the dark. The fish keep these bacteria on their sides or their spines.

The deep-sea angler fish has a small bulb at the end of a long spine which hangs in front of its mouth. The bulb contains bacteria which glow when they are given **oxygenated** blood. By changing the amount of oxygen in the blood, the fish can switch the light on and off. When it is switched on, it attracts smaller fish which the angler fish then swallows.

Flashlight fish use lights to help keep the shoal of fish together in the dark water. The lights are turned off if a predator appears so they cannot be seen.

The angler fish's bright bulb is attracting nearby smaller fish, so that it can eat them up

crustaceans: animals such as lobsters, shrimps, wood-lice and sand-hoppers

bacteria: very tiny, or microscopic organisms

oxygenated: containing lots of oxygen, which is a gas in air

Blood red

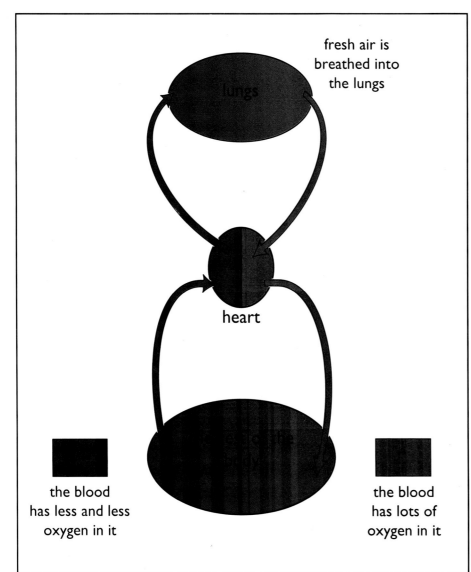

large white
blood cell

red blood cell
has a 'doughnut'
appearance

there are many more red blood
cells than white blood cells

fresh air is
breathed into
the lungs

lungs

heart

the blood
has less and less
oxygen in it

the blood
has lots of
oxygen in it

Our blood looks red. It seems to be a red liquid but it is really made up of two parts. The colour comes from blood cells which contain a special red pigment called haemoglobin. The red cells float in a yellow liquid called plasma. The haemoglobin is important because it can carry oxygen. An adult may have 5000 million red blood cells in 1 cubic millimetre of blood.

We all need oxygen in order to live. Blood flows around the body and as it does so it carries things from one part to another. One of the things it transports is oxygen. The blood flows through the lungs and the red blood cells pick up the oxygen which we have breathed in. The blood takes the oxygen to all parts of the body.

The job of carrying the blood around the body is done by the blood-vessels. These are small tubes. They carry the blood from the heart to all parts of the body and then bring it back again. The vessels which leave the heart and go to our cells are called arteries. The blood in arteries is bright red because it is carrying lots of oxygen. If you cut an artery the bright red blood will come spurting out, and it is very difficult to stop the flow.

Once the blood has reached our cells it has to go back to the heart, and then to the lungs to get more oxygen. It travels along another type of blood-vessel called a vein. Blood in veins does not contain much oxygen so the blood is a much darker red. The veins under the skin appear blue. Have a look at the veins near the surface of your skin on the underside of your arm. They should stand out as blue tubes.

Some babies are born with a hole in the heart. With this hole, the heart cannot pump enough blood to reach the lungs. Because the blood is not carrying much oxygen, it is much darker, and the skin all over the body looks blue. This is why these babies are called 'blue babies'. Fortunately, doctors can now repair such holes, and the babies regain their normal, healthy colour.

Usually, the skin of animals is pigmented or covered by fur or feathers, so it is not possible to see blood flowing within it. But in some animals, their red colouring is produced by blood showing through transparent, or see-through, skin. A well-known example is the comb and wattle of the cockerel.

A chicken's comb is actually transparent. The bright red colour is seen because the comb is full of blood

The axolotl, a type of salamander, has a white body and pink gills. The pink colour comes from the blood which flows through them

Inheriting colour

Even in animals of the same species, no two animals of different parents are ever exactly alike. If you look around your class you will recognize everyone. But though they are all humans, they are all slightly different.

If you look at a herd of cows, each one will have a slightly different coloured hide, or skin, from the others. We say they vary. The colours of each animal depend on the colours of its parents.

Many of our domesticated animals are specially bred for particular colours. We breed rabbits, dogs and other animals to get particular coat colours. Fish-breeders spend thousands of pounds on a specially coloured koi carp. They can then breed them to produce very special and rare colours and patterns. How do they do this?

COLOURFUL THINGS TO DO

Studying ladybirds in the garden

This project can only be carried out in the summer months when there are lots of ladybirds. The most common forms of ladybird that

you will find in your garden are the two-spot and the seven-spot. You now know why they have a bright red colour.

Make a collection of live ladybirds in your garden, or at school. Separate the two-spot species from the seven-spot. Study each species carefully. Are all the spots or patterns the same?

You will probably find that the seven-spot ladybirds have spots in almost the same positions on each of their bodies. The spots are also very similar in size on each of the bodies. But the two-spot is quite variable. The two-spot may have black wing-cases with red spots, or even stretchy spots. Make drawings of the different patterns you find.

Koi carp are specially bred for attractive colours and patterns. Some have rare colours and patterns, and can be very valuable

Labrador retrievers only have two very different coat colours, black and golden. They never produce puppies with a mixture of the two colours

The breeder picks out the animals with the most wanted colours and uses them to breed from. He hopes that the offspring will look like their parents. This is likely to happen, because the babies' cells contain genes, or sets of instructions from each parent. These instructions tell the offspring how to grow. They contain the exact details of colour, size and shape. Scientists call this passing on of instructions from parent to baby, genetics.

However, it is not always easy to tell what colour will result from two parents. Sometimes the babies are a different colour from what you might expect. Scientists can explain how colour, and other features, are passed down from parents to children through their genes. We will use dog-breeding as an example to explain simply how genetics works.

There are only two coat colours in the Labrador dog, gold and black. If a black and a golden Labrador breed, you may expect that half the puppies will be golden, and half, black. However, scientists have discovered that the genetic instructions passed down by the black colour are stronger than those of the golden colour. So, if a breeder crosses a golden Labrador with a black Labrador, all the offspring will be black. Why no golden ones? Well, because the genetic instructions for a black coat are stronger, they do not allow the golden coats to be produced. If a golden Labrador was mated with another golden Labrador, all the offspring would have golden coats.

Index

Books to read

Trials of Life David Attenborough (Collins/BBC Books)
Camouflage and Mimicry Jill Bailey (New Naturalist)
How Nature Works David Burnie (Dorling Kindersley)
Colours Ed Catherall (Wayland)
Discovery of Animal Behaviour John Sparks (Collins/BBC Books)